The
Black Death
1347–1350:

The plague spreads across Europe

CATH SENKER

www.raintreepublishers.co.uk

Visit our website to find out more information about **Raintree** books.

To order:

 Phone 44 (0) 1865 888113

Send a fax to 44 (0) 1865 314091

Visit the Raintree bookshop at **www.raintreepublishers.co.uk**
to browse our catalogue and order online.

First published in Great Britain by Raintree, Halley Court, Jordan Hill, Oxford OX2 8EJ, part of Harcourt Education.

Raintree is a registered trademark of Harcourt Education Ltd.

Editorial: Andrew Farrow and Christine Mc Cafferty
Design: Victoria Bevan and AMR Design Ltd
Illustrations: David Woodroffe
Picture Research: Maria Joannou and
    Ginny Stroud-Lewis
Production: Chloe Bloom

Originated by Modern Age
Printed and bound in China by South
    China Printing Company

10 digit ISBN 1 406 20286 X
13 digit ISBN 978 1 4062 0286 1

10 09 08 07 06
10 9 8 7 6 5 4 3 2 1

British Library Cataloguing in Publication Data
Senker, Cath
Black Death, 1347. - (When disaster struck)
614.5'732'09023

A full catalogue record for this book is available from the British Library.

Acknowledgements

The publishers would like to thank the following for permission to reproduce photographs:

AKG Images p.22 (VISIOARS); Alamy pp.17 (Che Garman), 39 (Bildarchiv Monheim GmbH); Corbis pp.4 (Bettmann), 13 (MAPS.com), 41 (Bettmann), 43 (Hulton-Deutsch Collection), 47 (Kapoor Baldev/Sygma), 48 (Bettmann); Getty Images pp.32 (Hulton Archive), 45 (Time & Life Pictures); Mary Evans Picture Library pp.33, 35; Scala Archives p.32; The Art Archive pp.12 (Biblioteca Nazionale Marciana Venice/Dagli Orti), 14 (Cathedral Perugia/Dagli Orti), 16 (Palazzo Pubblico Siena/Dagli Orti), 19 (University Library Prague/Dagli Orti), 21 (Saint Sebastian Chapel Lanslevillard Savoy/Dagli Orti), 26 (Bibliothèque Nationale Paris), 27 (University Library Prague/ Dagli Orti), 36 (Musée du Petit Palais Avignon/ Dagli Orti), 46; The Bridgeman Art Library pp.6 (Bibliotheque Nationale, Paris, France Giraudon), 9 (©The Barnes Foundation, Merion, Pennsylvania, USA), 10-11 (Scuola Grande di San Rocco, Venice, Italy), 20 (Private Collection, Ken Welsh), 25 (Bibliotheque Mazarine, Paris, France, Archives Charmet), 28 (© Walters Art Museum, Baltimore, USA), 42 (Musee du Berry, Bourges, France, Lauros/Giraudon).

Cover illustration of a man carrying a child suffering from the plague, reproduced with permission of Mary Evans Picture Library.

The publishers would like to thank Philip Ziegler for his assistance in the preparation of this book.

BLOOD, BOILS, AND DEATH

It is October 1347. At the port of Messina in Sicily, southern Italy, twelve Genoese trading ships arrive at the harbour.

The sailors get off the **galleys**. Local traders and fishermen watch as the **Genoese** crews collapse. They are suffering from a terrible disease.

Immediately, the people of Messina fall ill. The city quickly sends the Genoese galleys away. But it is too late. The Black Death has arrived in Europe.

Friar Michele from Messina wrote, "a sort of boil [...] erupted on the thigh or arm. Then the victims violently coughed up blood. After three days of constant vomiting [...] they died. And with them died everyone who had talked to them. Anyone who touched or laid hands on their belongings died too." Over the next four years, the Black Death would sweep across the continent.

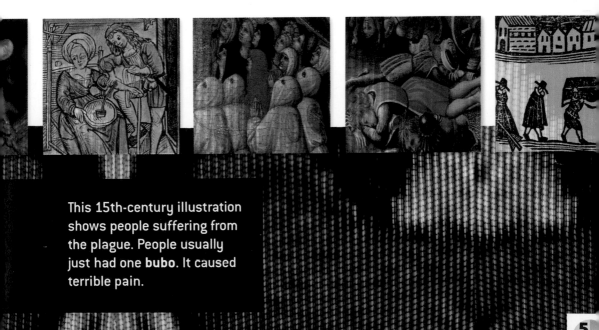

This 15th-century illustration shows people suffering from the plague. People usually just had one **bubo**. It caused terrible pain.

THE DEADLY PLAGUE

The Black Death, 1347–1350

PLAGUE OUTBREAK

The plague probably broke out in the early 1300s in inner Asia.

Historians and scientists believe it might have started around Lake Issyk Kul, which is in modern-day Kyrgyzstan. This lake is close to several places where the plague occurs in nature.

A Russian **archaeologist**, D. A. Chwolson, found evidence of a very high death rate near the lake. He found an unusually large number of headstones in local cemeteries. One of them read: "In the year of the hare (1330) This is the grave of Kutluk. He died of the plague with his wife Magnu-Kelka." From the area of the lake, the plague spread east to China and west to the Middle East and Europe.

As merchants travelled on business, they spread the plague along their trade routes. It spread both over land and sea.

CATASTROPHE FROM CHINA TO EUROPE

In the 1330s China suffered rains, droughts, and earthquakes. At the same time, the plague began to spread. Chinese records from 1331 describe a mysterious illness that swept through Hopei province in the northeast. It killed 90 per cent of the population. An Arab scholar, Ibn al-Wardi, said that the plague raged for 15 years in the East before it spread to Europe.

The **chronicler** of Este, in Italy, described the shocking spread of death in the East in the mid-1340s. He did not understand what really caused it:

"Between Cathay (China) and Persia (Iran) there rained a vast rain of fire. The fire fell in flakes like snow. It burnt up mountains and plains and other lands. Men and women died too. Then vast masses of smoke arose. Anyone who saw the smoke died within half a day; and likewise any man or woman who looked upon those who had seen this (also died)."

The plague travelled west through Asia. In 1346 it spread to cities near the Caspian Sea. A year later it reached Kaffa (now Feodosiya), an important trade centre on the Black Sea. As the people who lived in Kaffa began to die of the plague, the merchants boarded ships to sail home to Europe. From Kaffa, and perhaps other ports, the Genoese galleys brought the plague (also called the pestilence) to Europe.

WHY WAS IT CALLED THE BLACK DEATH?

Many people think that the plague was called the Black Death because a person's flesh turned black before they died. But this did not happen. In the 1340s, Europeans did not call the plague Black Death. They called it the "Big Death" or "Great Mortality". The words "Black Death" were first written down in 1555. Historians believe this comes from the translation of the Latin words *atra mors*. These words mean "terrible death" or "black death".

This painting from the 1400s shows three saints. The saint in the middle is Saint Roch. The bubo on his thigh shows that he suffered from the plague.

INTO ITALY AND FRANCE

The plague spread across the island of Sicily. Messina is on the northern side of Sicily, where it meets the mainland of Italy. In autumn 1347, hundreds of people in Messina were dying every day. Any contact with an infected person seemed to spread the disease and bring certain death.

The people of Messina panicked. Friar Michele described how, "The disease bred such hatred that if a son fell ill[...] his father flatly refused to stay with him." Many people ran away to other parts of Sicily. But they just carried the disease with them. Within a year about 33 per cent of Sicilians may have died. By late 1347 the Black Death reached mainland Italy.

Another chronicler described the arrival of the plague at the port of Genoa in northern Italy. He wrote that in January 1348, three galleys reached Genoa from the East. They were carrying spices and other goods. The sailors were infected with a horrible disease. The sailors rapidly infected local people.

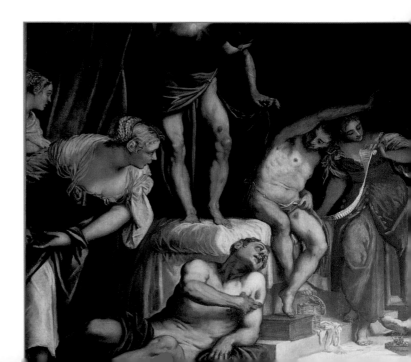

The Genoese were horrified. The chronicler wrote, "The Genoese drove them away from that port with fiery arrows and engines of war. For no man dared touch them. If any man traded with the crew, he would die straight away. Thus, the galleys were scattered from port to port."

The sailors on the plague-infected galleys were desperate for food and water. One crew managed to sail to Marseille in France. The ship arrived in November 1347.

It took the local people completely by surprise. One of the townspeople said, "Men were infected without realizing it and died suddenly. The inhabitants then drove the galley away." But the plague had already taken hold. After Marseille, the plague spread north through France. In summer 1348 it reached Paris and Normandy.

Meanwhile, the plague spread through Genoa, Venice, and the cities of central Italy. Around 33 per cent of Italians died.

This painting from Venice shows Saint Roch curing the plague. Many people prayed to saints for a miracle cure.

ITALIAN CITIES RAVAGED

In January 1348 the disease reached the island city of Venice in Italy. The city council worked fast to try to stop the spread of infection. All ships entering Venice were searched. If there were foreigners or corpses aboard, the ship was set on fire.

Boatmen sailed past all the houses in the city, collecting the dead bodies of plague victims to get rid of them.

In March Florence was hit and in August, Rome. In Florence, the writer Giovanni Boccaccio described how some people simply "deserted their city, their houses, their estates".

This illustration from the 1300s shows the people of Venice taking their dead to be buried. By June 1348, nearly 600 people were dying every day in Venice.

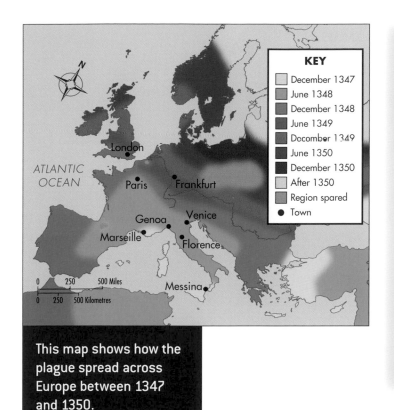

KEY

December 1347
June 1348
December 1348
June 1349
December 1349
June 1350
December 1350
After 1350
Region spared
● Town

ATLANTIC
OCEAN

London

Paris   Frankfurt

Genoa   Venice

Marseille   Florence

Messina

0   250   500 Miles
0   250   500 Kilometres

This map shows how the plague spread across Europe between 1347 and 1350.

PLACES REACHED BY THE BLACK DEATH IN EUROPE

1347 The Crimea, Greece, Sicily, Sardinia, Corsica, France

1348 Italy, southern England, Spain, Austria, Ireland

1349 southern Germany, Portugal, central and northern England, Wales, Norway, Sweden, Denmark, the Netherlands

1350 Scotland, northern Germany, Poland

1352 Russia

Boccaccio said they left the city or moved to the countryside, "as if God would not pursue them". The plague affected both rich and poor people. But it was easier for rich people to escape to other areas.

In some Italian cities, sensible practices slowed down the spread of the plague. In Venice, removing all the dead bodies quickly helped. In Milan, citizens walled up the homes of those infected with plague, trapping both sick and healthy people inside to die.

HOW MANY DIED?

Nobody knows exactly how many people died in the Black Death. Medieval writers were not able to give accurate figures. They often claimed there were far more deaths than there really were. These figures are very rough estimates.

Country	Estimated percentage of the population who died
Spain	60–65 %
Italy	50–60 %
France	60 %
England	62.5 %

HORROR
AND
HYSTERIA

The Black Death, 1347–1350

TYPES OF PLAGUE

Medieval Europeans could not understand why some people survived the plague for several days, while others died in a day or two. Some even died in hours.

There were in fact three different forms of the plague: **bubonic**, **pneumonic**, and **septicaemic**. The bubonic plague was spread by fleas. It made the **lymph glands** in the groin or armpit swell to form buboes.

Pneumonic plague attacked the lungs and was the most infectious of the three kinds. It could spread directly from person to person through coughing. The bubonic and pneumonic forms were most common.

The rarest and most dangerous form was septicaemic plague. Spread by fleas, it rapidly attacked the bloodstream. People dropped dead in hours. Boccaccio wrote how the victims, "ate breakfast with their friends and dinner with their **ancestors** in paradise".

People hurry to leave the city of Perugia to escape the plague.

RATS, FLEAS, AND DISEASE

How did the Black Death spread? The answer lies with the tiny rat flea. Rat fleas carried the plague **bacillus** — a type of bacteria. The fleas jumped on to rats and other rodents and infected them with the plague. When their **host** died, they leapt on to another rat. Once the local rats had died, the fleas fed on human beings. They spread the plague to their human hosts.

Medieval European cities were very dirty. Butchers killed animals on the street and left the blood there. Piles of unwanted **offal** littered the ground. People emptied their **chamber pots** out of their windows. Human **excrement** and urine covered the streets.

In this Italian painting from the 1300s, animals can be seen carrying goods to market. Few people in medieval times cleared up the animal dung, so the streets were dirty.

These are black rats. Black rats carried the plague. Medieval people were used to seeing rats everywhere. They did not realize that rats spread the disease.

The dirty cities were the perfect place for rats. There was a good food supply. The rats fed on people's stored grains and food scraps. Also, rats could move freely. Most people lived in narrow rows of houses crammed together. The lanes between the rows were so narrow that rats could easily run between homes. Infected rats quickly spread the plague.

The plague spread fast in the countryside, too. The walls in country homes were so thin that rats could gnaw through from house to house.

Medieval people did not keep their homes or themselves clean. Many shared their homes with their pigs, horses, chickens, and goats. They did not believe in washing. In fact they thought bathing was bad for a person's health. They seldom undressed or changed their clothes. People's dirty bodies were crawling with fleas. Fleas were able to jump quickly from person to person, spreading the plague.

RAT BABIES!

Rats are very good at spreading disease. They breed fast and are very mobile. It is calculated that if two black rats bred for three years (and none of the babies died) they and their offspring could produce 329 million babies in that time. Rats can climb walls, squeeze through tiny gaps, and survive a fall from 15 metres (49 feet). They can gnaw through most surfaces – even lead pipes.

BLOODLETTING AND STINKS

Medieval Europeans tried all kinds of things to prevent the plague spreading. People rang church bells, wore lucky charms, or bathed in urine.

European doctors had no idea how the plague spread. Many believed it was caused by poisonous air. They told people to fill their houses with pleasant-smelling plants and flowers. Some doctors burned sweet-smelling herbs to clear the air.

One doctor, John Colle, thought sniffing bad smells would protect people from catching the plague. Some people spent hours crouching over a filthy public **latrine**, breathing in the disgusting smells. Others put "stinks" (dead animals) in their homes.

Some physicians **lanced** people's buboes. This was very painful. Others washed their patients in vinegar or rose water. They told them to avoid strong-tasting foods. Many **physicians** thought **bloodletting** would help. Others gave out herbal remedies.

A Swedish bishop, Bengt Knutsson, said people should avoid bathing. He thought that washing opened the pores in the body and allowed the disease to enter. None of these practices were helpful.

Some physicians suggested eating a good diet. This idea was sensible because good food strengthens the body against disease.

A few people did survive bubonic plague. After days of terrible pain, their buboes burst, and pus poured out. They gradually recovered.

Most people realized that contact with someone with the plague, or even with his clothing, was dangerous. Some were even scared of a sufferer looking at them!

There were reports of people leaving their loved ones to die painful, lonely deaths. They were fearful of catching the plague themselves. In Avignon in France, a musician called Louis Heyligen complained, "Everyone who is healthy looks only after himself."

Others helped the sick, although at risk to their own lives. One story tells of Simonia, a kind woman in Genoa. She nursed her friend Aminigina until she died, ignoring the danger to herself. Some monks in Avignon cared for plague victims. They fed them, washed their bodies, and eased the pain of their buboes. Most of the monks soon died of plague themselves.

A doctor is using bloodletting to try to cure the plague. He cuts the patient's arm and allows some blood to flow into a bowl.

PANIC IN FLORENCE

Giovanni Boccaccio witnessed the plague first hand. He described how people in Florence reacted to the plague. Some small groups shut themselves away from society. They enjoyed fine foods and wines, listened to music, and took part in pleasant pastimes.

Other people did not cut themselves off from society. They drank day and night in the taverns, laughed, and made merry. Some people roamed the town, but tried to be careful. When walking around, they sniffed perfumes or herbs to avoid breathing in the smells of the dead and dying.

Giovanni Boccaccio was shocked that his fellow citizens left their adult relatives to their fate. "But even worse was the fact that fathers and mothers refused to nurse and assist their own children, as though they did not belong to them." Some people left parents, husbands, wives, and children who had caught the plague.

TWO PIGS DIE

Boccaccio told how the rags of a poor man who had died of the plague were thrown into the street. Two pigs came along and smelt the rags with their snouts. They then took the rags between their teeth and tossed them around. Almost immediately, they gave a few turns, and fell down dead.

Boccaccio lived through the plague in Florence and wrote about the experience. His book, *The Decameron*, is still well known.

In this 15th-century **fresco**, a man prays to Saint Sebastian to protect him from the plague. People believed he could heal buboes.

The lawyer Gabriele de' Mussis of Piacenza, in Italy, wrote, "When one person lay sick in a house no one would come near. Even dear friends would hide themselves away weeping. The physician would not visit." The priest, trembling with fear, came to say the special prayers for the dying person.

In Italy it had been the custom for female mourners to come to the house of the victim. They would then accompany the coffin to the graveyard. Now there were few mourners.

The victims were not buried in their own grave but in vast plague pits. Marchione di Coppo Stefani, from Florence, said the dead were placed "layer upon layer just like one puts layers of cheese on lasagna".

SOCIETY IN CRISIS

The Black Death, 1347–1350

CATTLE WANDERING

In June 1348 the monks of Saint Denis reported that in Paris 800 people were dying everyday.

The disease travelled northwards to the French coast. It also spread northeast towards the Netherlands.

A Benedictine **abbot**, Gilles Li Muisis wrote, "It is almost impossible to believe the death through the whole country. Travellers, merchants, pilgrims, and others [...] declare that they have found cattle wandering without herdsmen in the fields, towns, and wastelands. They have seen barns and wine cellars standing wide open, houses empty, and few people to be found anywhere."

The abbot said that rich people had a better chance of survival than the poor. But he noted, "no one was secure, whether rich or poor. Everyone, from day to day, waited on the will of the Lord."

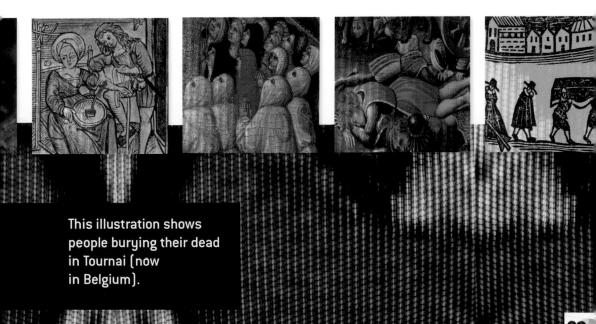

This illustration shows people burying their dead in Tournai (now in Belgium).

PERSECUTION AND TERROR

In 1348 the plague swept across France and modern-day Switzerland. It reached Germany in summer 1349. Most people believed that the horror was God's will.

Other people blamed the Jews. They accused them of poisoning the wells to infect Christians with the plague. In some places, Jewish people were arrested. They were forced to confess to the crime of poisoning.

As a punishment, mobs began **pogroms**. They killed entire Jewish communities, stole their property, and burned their homes. Sometimes they told the Jews they would save them if they gave up their religion and converted to Christianity. Most Jews chose death.

The Jews were safe in one place in southern France. The people of Marseille left the Jewish community of 2,500 people in peace. Jewish people fled to Marseille from other towns in France to escape attack.

The pogroms began in Germany in November 1348. The plague had not even arrived yet. In January 1349, the people of Speyer murdered Jews. They threw their dead bodies into wine casks. They tossed the casks into the River Rhine.

In the same month, the people of Basel in Switzerland forced all the Jews into wooden buildings. Then they set fire to the buildings and burned them alive. The **persecution** of the Jews continued as the plague spread through Europe.

BURNT ALIVE

A churchman called Heinrich Truchess described the murders of Jews in Germany in 1349:

"On 4 January the people of Constance shut up the Jews in two of their own houses. Then they burnt 330 of them in the fields at sunset on 3 March. Some proceeded into the flames dancing, others singing, and the rest weeping."

The plague was also terrifying for children. If their parents died, there was often no one to care for them. They had to look after themselves. Children saw death and destruction all around them.

In Norway the people of a remote village tried to stay away from others to avoid getting the plague. Despite this, the disease reached them. Legend has it that the plague killed all who lived there, except one little girl. Later, a rescue party found the survivor. The girl had been alone for months and was living like a wild animal.

This **woodcut** from 1493 shows Jewish people being burned alive. The Jews had often suffered persecution. Their sufferings were particularly bad during the Black Death.

LOOKING FOR THE CAUSE

The Black Death hit Europe at the time of the Hundred Years' War between England and France (1337–1453). Large areas of France were already suffering because of the war. Many crops and animals had been destroyed or stolen. The French **peasants** did not have enough to eat. They were weak and fell ill easily. This is one reason why people died in such large numbers from the plague.

People at the time did not understand the real reasons for the plague. Most people agreed the plague was a punishment from God for their sins. There were some who blamed greedy traders, and priests who were more interested in money than serving God. Others blamed people who wore tight clothes.

This painting shows the Battle of Blanchetaque. It was fought between the English and the French armies in 1346. Many people in England and France were suffering because of the Hundred Years' war.

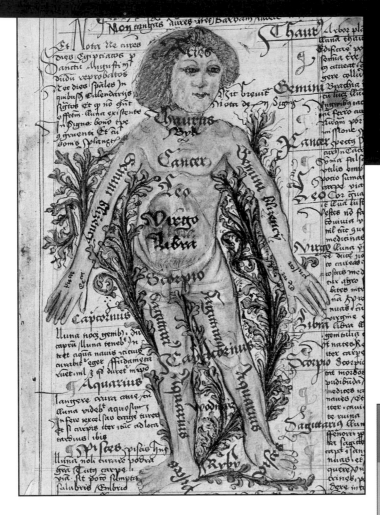

This illustration from a 15th-century treatise shows how the stars were supposed to influence the human body.

Others looked to **astrology** to explain the plague. Some medical people in Paris, France, wrote a plague **treatise** in 1348. They noted that the planets Mars, Jupiter, and Saturn passed close together in 1345. They thought it was possible this event had brought disaster with it.

Some were certain that the earthquakes, floods, tidal waves, and unusual weather in the 1330s and 1340s had helped cause the plague.

A writer in the early 1360s thought that children suffered badly in the plague outbreak of 1361 because they did not obey their parents.

THE BODIES PILE HIGH

The Black Death, 1347–1350

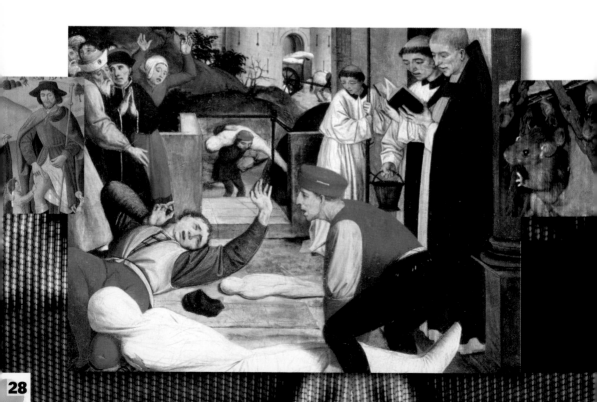

DEATH IN ENGLAND

In summer 1348, the Bishop of Bath and Wells in southern England warned his fellow Englishmen to pray to God to stop the plague spreading to England.

However, it did not stop. Historians believe the plague probably first hit Melcombe, a village in southwest England.

Henry Knighton from Leicester wrote in his **chronicle**, "The most terrible plague attacked the coast through Southampton and came to Bristol. Nearly the whole town was wiped out. It was as if sudden death had marked them down beforehand. Few lay sick for more than two or three days, or even for half a day. Cruel death took just two days to burst out all over a town."

Over the next two years, England was to suffer the worst disaster in its history.

In this late 15th-century painting, Saint Sebastian pleads with God to have mercy on the people who are suffering from plague.

LONDON IS STRUCK

Bristol was the first major town to be affected. It was a busy trading port. About 10,000 people lived there, crowded together. It is not surprising the plague spread fast. After hitting Bristol, the plague raced across southwest England. The English people were struck with panic and fear.

In autumn 1348, the plague reached London. London was the most important city in the country. It was the centre of industry and business. About 60,000 to 100,000 people lived inside the city walls.

London was a filthy city. Rich people had toilets that stuck out over the River Thames. The contents of the toilets gushed down into the river.

Everyone threw their rubbish straight on to the streets. There were gutters in the middle of the streets to carry away the litter. These gutters often became blocked.

King Edward III realised the filth was a problem. He wrote a letter to the Mayor of London in 1349. He said, "You are to make sure that all the human excrement and other filth lying in the street of the city is removed. You are to cause the city to be cleaned from all bad smells so that no more people will die from such smells." Unfortunately, most of the street cleaners had already died of plague.

The Black Death spread rapidly through the narrow streets and crowded homes. Food sellers soon refused to enter the city. People had little to eat.

Many Londoners went to the countryside in search of food. In this way they spread the plague.

APPROXIMATE DATES OF THE SPREAD OF THE PLAGUE IN THE BRITISH ISLES:

1348
June: Plague arrives in Melcombe, south coast (now Weymouth)
August: Bristol
September: London
October: Winchester

1349
January–February: East Anglia
April: Wales
July: Ireland
Autumn: Durham

1350
Spring: Scotland

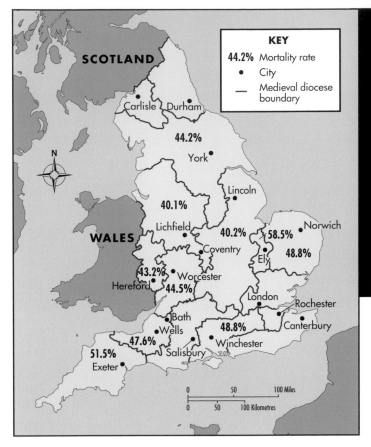

KEY

44.2% Mortality rate
• City
— Medieval diocese boundary

SCOTLAND

Carlisle   Durham

44.2%
York

Lincoln

40.1%

Lichfield   40.2%   58.5%   Norwich
WALES   Coventry   Ely   48.8%

43.2%   Worcester
Hereford   44.5%

London   Rochester
Bath   Canterbury
Wells   48.8%
47.6%   Winchester
51.5%   Salisbury
Exeter

0   50   100 Miles
0   50   100 Kilometres

We do not know exactly how many people died in England during the Black Death. Records of the deaths of English parish priests give a rough idea. In many medieval churches, you can see a list of the priests. There are often quite a few who died between 1347 and 1350.

The plague now spread in all directions. It moved northwards through England to Durham.

The Scots were delighted that their English enemies had fallen to the disease. They were just about to invade England when they too were attacked by the plague. The chronicler Henry Knighton wrote, "Within a short space of time, around 5,000 of them had died, and the rest, weak and strong alike, decided to retreat to their own country." In panic, the soldiers rushed home, and spread the disease to Scotland.

Geoffrey the Baker wrote how the plague then "laid waste the Welsh as well as the English, and then it took ship to Ireland." By the end of 1350, all of Britain had been infected by the disease.

DEALING WITH THE DEAD

In normal times, a priest came to hear a dying person **confess** his or her sins. The priest gave the last rites – the prayers for the dying. Because they gave comfort to the sick, priests ran a high risk of catching the plague themselves. So many priests died that there was a big shortage of them.

In western England, Bishop Ralph of Shrewsbury said, "If people who fall sick cannot find a priest, then they should make a confession to each other."

People were dying in huge numbers. The graveyards quickly filled up. At the beginning of 1349, the plague was raging in London. Two new graveyards were hurriedly opened to make space to bury the bodies.

This artwork, created in the 1800s, shows people praying for help during the Black Death.

RING-A-ROUND THE ROSY

It is said that during the Black Death, English children used to recite the poem "Ring-a-round the rosy".
It describes death from the plague. This is one version of the poem:

"Ring-a-round the rosy
Pocket full of posies
Ashes, ashes! We all fall down!"
Historians believe that the poem could have a variety of meanings.

This is one possible meaning:
Use the rosary beads to pray. Hold flowers to cover up the smell of rotting bodies. We burn the dead bodies when there are too many to bury. We fall down dead.

RINGEL-REIHN.

E.W.

William Dene was a monk in Rochester, southern England. He reported that the plague killed so many people that nobody could be found to carry the corpses to the grave. "Men and women carried their own children on their shoulders to the church and threw them into a common pit. From these pits an appalling stench was given off. Scarcely anyone dared even to walk beside the cemeteries."

Children carried on playing "ring-a-round the rosy" long after the Black Death. *Ringel Reihn* means "ring-a-round the rosy" in German.

MADNESS AND MASSACRES

The Black Death, 1347–1350

DISEASE MOVES ON

By 1349 the plague had spread to Norway, Denmark, Sweden, Scotland, Ireland, Austria, Germany, and the Netherlands.

Denmark was the most powerful country in Scandinavia and had the largest population. The Danish *Chronicle of Zealand* states that in 1349 "there was a great mortality in Denmark". Perhaps 33 per cent of the population died.

Greenland had a cold climate and a small, scattered population. The disease even managed to spread there.

With the plague causing chaos all over Europe, there were some extreme reactions to it. There were attacks on Jews. The **Flagellant** movement also arose. It began in 1348 in eastern Europe, and was especially popular in Germany.

This illustration shows people burying their dead in Norway in 1349. Ships sailing from England brought the plague to Norway.

THE FLAGELLANTS

Members of the Flagellant movement marched from town to town, usually in groups of 200 to 300. All wore red crosses on their clothes. Often they camped in fields near towns. Large numbers of people flocked to welcome them.

After arriving in a town, the Flagellants formed a large circle. They stripped to the waist and marched around the circle. Then they flung themselves to the ground. The Flagellants began to beat themselves with whips. They whipped themselves into a frenzy.

By punishing themselves, they hoped God would have mercy on them. He might stop the plague.

This is a group of Flagellants, kneeling in prayer before they start to whip themselves.

A 1349 account described the whips the Flagellants used, "Each whip was made from a stick with three knotted thongs hanging from the end. Two pieces of metal ran through the centre of the knots from both sides, forming a cross. Using these whips they beat and whipped their bare skin until their bodies were bruised and swollen. Blood rained down, spattering the walls nearby."

The Flagellants travelled around Hungary, Poland, Flanders, and modern-day Belgium, Luxembourg, and the Netherlands. There were many of them. One monastery had to provide for 2,500 Flagellants within six months!

In October 1349, Pope Clement VI said that they were not following Church rules. Their actions had to stop. Many of them were **excommunicated** from the Church. By 1350 the movement had vanished.

FOLLOWING THE FLAGELLANTS

Members of the Flagellants had to follow strict rules. They had to:

- confess to all sins committed since the age of 7
- promise to whip themselves 3 times daily for 33 days and 8 hours
- sleep on straw
- pay for the cost of their food on their journey, although this was not much as many villagers gave them food
- obey their leader.

All Flagellants also had to agree not to shave, bath, or change their clothes. They could not talk or have anything to do with the opposite sex during their march.

THE JEWS AND HYGIENE

While the Flagellants were on the march, the massacres of Jews continued. The Flagellants hated Jews and often murdered whole communities. In most cities the people killed the Jews once the plague had arrived. Sometimes, even the news that the plague was on the way led to attacks.

In February 1349 in Strasbourg (in modern-day France), a mob tore the clothes from Jews. Then the attackers murdered about 2,000 of them. In the German cities of Frankfurt, Mainz, and Cologne, there were further massacres in the summer. In Mainz around 12,000 Jewish people were killed.

Most European rulers made some efforts to protect the Jews, especially Pope Clement VI. In July 1348, the pope pointed out that, "It cannot be true that the Jews are the cause of the plague for it afflicts the Jews themselves." He called on Christians to be tolerant of the Jews. The leaders had little success though. Because of the violent attacks, Jewish communities in large areas of Europe were completely wiped out.

One of the reasons the Jews were persecuted was the belief that fewer of them were dying. This might have been because the Jews had a better understanding of hygiene than most people. In the Jewish *Torah* (holy book), in the writings of Moses, there are instructions about how to keep towns clean and stop the spread of disease.

The Jews realized that many wells in towns were dirty because there were **sewage pits** nearby. They therefore preferred to fetch drinking water from open streams, rather than wells. This could be the reason why other people thought they were poisoning the wells, and so persecuted them.

In the few places where there was good hygiene, it was more difficult for the plague to take hold. The priory (building where monks and nuns lived) at Christ Church in the city of Canterbury, England, had a good water supply and drainage system. The building was clean and free of rats. Only four people died of the plague there.

The priory and convent of Christ Church was attached to Canterbury Cathedral. Christ Church had drainage pipes that helped keep the priory clean and so largely free of the plague.

THE CULTURE OF DEATH

The Black Death, 1347–1350

DANCE OF DEATH

The Black Death raged throughout Europe until 1353, by which time about 33 per cent of the European population had died.

There were further deaths in the Caucasus, Asia Minor, the Middle East, and North Africa. With so much death in people's lives, European culture became very gloomy. The "Dance of Death" was a popular theme among painters and writers. Death was shown at parties, dancing with all the party-goers, both rich and poor.

Some people did in fact dance to try keep their fears at bay. In a chronicle by Saint Denis from Paris, a man says, "We have seen our neighbours die and see them die daily. But since the plague has not entered our town, we hope our merrymaking will keep it away. That is why we dance."

Around Europe people gathered to dance in the hope that they could keep the plague away from their village.

PLAGUE SURVIVORS

In 1352–1353 the plague spread through Russia. Russia was close to the part of inner Asia where the disease had started. The plague had now gone full circle. It had swept all around Europe and parts of Asia, northern Africa, and the Middle East. The survivors were **immune** to the disease. It could not spread any more – for the time being.

When the plague had finally disappeared, people celebrated. They ate delicious food, drank wildly, and gambled. The birth rate rose. French monk Jean de Venette noticed that "there were pregnant women wherever you looked". People enjoyed having time to do what they wanted.

Yet the survivors still felt terrible grief. They had a strong fear of death and thought about it all the time. Artists produced paintings showing human suffering and the tortures of hell. Death was often one of the main characters.

ESTIMATED POPULATION OF EUROPE

Year	Population
1200	59 million
1300	70 million
1347	75 million
1352	50 million

This is a painting called the *Triumph of Death*. This kind of painting was very common at the time. You can sense how much people thought about death and feared it.

Another result of the Black Death was that many people lost faith in the Catholic Church and the saints. They had not been able to protect them when they needed help. They felt let down. Many of the best priests had died in the plague. The Church took on new priests, but they were not well educated. Many people did not respect them.

Yet somehow the structure of society held together. In fact the dramatic loss of life helped Europe in some ways. There were now more resources, such as houses and land, for the survivors. In the countryside, many **tenant farmers** were likely to have a larger land holding (more land they could rent and use). They took over land from their neighbours who had died.

Many young people of working age had died. There was therefore a huge shortage of people to work the land. Labourers could demand higher wages. Landowners offered extras such as food, drink, and other benefits to get labourers to work for them. People had more freedom to choose the work they wanted to do.

The shortage of workers affected industry, too. It eventually led to new ways of making things that needed fewer workers.

This is an ossuary. It is a room where the bones of the dead are kept. This ossuary in Poland holds the bones of plague victims.

"WALLOWING IN LAZINESS"

Matteo Villani from Florence, Italy, believed that the plague survivors were ungrateful to God. He wrote:

"It was thought that people whom God had saved would become better, humble and good. But the opposite happened. Men wallowed in laziness. They were led into the sins of greed and gambling."

DISEASE AND REBELLION

The plague returned in 1361. It killed so many children and teenagers that it is often called the "children's plague". Most of those children were born after the last plague outbreak. They did not have the immunity that the older survivors had.

An unknown writer from Canterbury described the new wave of deaths throughout the world: "In England the pestilence began in June that year. Children and teenagers were generally the first to die, and then the elderly. Members of religious orders and parish clergy and others died suddenly. Many churches were then left empty through lack of priests."

As well as further outbreaks of plague, Europe suffered from other diseases. There were outbreaks of **smallpox**, **influenza**, **dysentery**, and **typhus**.

Because of the deaths from disease, wages for the survivors continued to rise. One group in particular gained after the plague – women. Some took on well-paid jobs such as metalwork and weaving. Widows took over family shops and businesses. Historians have shown that they often ran them better than their husbands had.

However, the general increase in wages was a big problem for the wealthy classes. In England King Edward III (1327–1377) brought in new laws. The new laws lowered wages to the same level as before the plague. Peasants were not allowed to change jobs.

The king also extended a tax called the **poll tax** to the poorest people. His attempt to put the peasants down was one cause of the Peasants' Revolt in 1381. Similar peasants' rebellions erupted in Europe at around the same time.

Europe was not only hit by rebellion. There were further plague outbreaks, in 1379–83, 1389–93, throughout the first half of the 1400s, and beyond.

It seemed that Europe would never be completely rid of the terrible pestilence. But none of the outbreaks were as severe as the first terrible Black Death of 1347–1350. Gradually, European countries introduced laws to keep their towns and cities cleaner.

England was slow to adopt rules to protect people's health. The first laws were introduced in the 1500s. In several towns in the late 1530s, people infected with plague were shut away in special houses outside the city walls.

In 1563 London experienced yet another plague outbreak. Many rich people fled to the country. Queen Elizabeth I and her court moved to Windsor Castle. She ordered that anyone coming from London to Windsor be hanged.

The anger of English peasants over wage cuts and taxes led to the Peasants' Revolt of 1381. Wat Tyler was the leader of the revolt. Here, he is shown in a battle against King Richard II. In the end, he had his head cut off by the mayor of London.

FIGHTING PLAGUE

When the plague broke out in 1578, Queen Elizabeth again took action. She brought out detailed orders to stop infection spreading. Many public gatherings were outlawed. All bars and theatres were ordered to close.

By this time, people had learnt to keep away from plague sufferers and their belongings. They lit fires in the hope that it would clear the air of infection.

By the 1600s, it was mostly the poorer areas of towns and cities that suffered badly from the plague. Here people still lived in filthy, overcrowded places where there were lots of rats.

The plague hit London in 1665. It was most severe in the poor quarters of the city. This page from a London newspaper of 1665 shows bodies being taken for burial. Death, at the bottom of the picture, is victorious again.

The plague did not die out completely in Europe until the 1720s. In 1894, it struck Canton and Hong Kong in South China. Within 20 years the pestilence spread across the whole world. It left more than 10 million dead.

It was during this outbreak that Japanese and French scientists discovered the bacillus that causes the plague. Later, researchers finally worked out that the plague was spread by rats and fleas. In 1932 an effective treatment was developed to treat the disease. When plague broke out in India in 1994, treatment with **antibiotics** saved many lives.

Plague lives on in Asia today. Surprisingly it is also found in the United States, spread by rodents such as squirrels and chipmunks. Very few Americans – only 10 to 20 people each year – catch the disease. They are cured with antibiotics.

During the plague outbreak in Surat, India, in 1994, people queue up to get medicine to stop them catching the disease. They cover their faces to avoid spreading germs.

PLAGUES IN OUR TIME

Many deadly diseases have afflicted our modern world.

SPANISH FLU

In 1918–1919, Spanish flu killed between 20 and 40 million people. A doctor in Massachusetts, United States, described soldiers suffering from Spanish flu, "These men start with what seems to be an ordinary attack of influenza. They very rapidly develop the most vicious type of **pneumonia** that has ever been seen. Two hours after coming to hospital they have the mahogany spots over the cheek bones. A few hours later you can begin to see the cyanosis (blueish tinge because of a lack of oxygen). It is only a matter of a few hours then until death comes. They struggle for air until they die."

This photo from about 1917 shows nurses caring for victims of Spanish flu in an outdoor hospital. Spanish flu killed more people than had died during the whole of the First World War (1914–1918).

AIDS

In 1981 AIDS was first reported. AIDS attacks the body's defence system. The patient catches other diseases easily and eventually dies. It is estimated that between 36 and 44 million people are living with HIV, the **virus** that causes AIDS. About 60 per cent of them are in sub-Saharan Africa. There is no cure for AIDS and millions have already died. Treatment to help people live longer exists, but most people cannot afford it.

BSE – "MAD COW DISEASE"

BSE is a brain disease that was first discovered in UK cattle in 1986. It was reported in other parts of Europe and Canada. Infected animals lose control of their muscles and usually die within a year. It seems that feeding methods caused BSE. Cattle are normally vegetarian. But they were fed the offal of other animals. The human form of the disease is called new variant Creutzfeld-Jacob disease. It has killed dozens of people in Europe. There is no known cure.

SARS

In November 2002, a serious breathing disease called SARS appeared in China. It caused panic in major cities in Asia. By May 2003, about 800 people had died. The authorities immediately stopped people travelling to and from affected countries. They isolated infected people. With these measures, they controlled SARS.

All these diseases are terrifying. They could wipe out millions of people. AIDS already has. There is still no cure, although it can be prevented. Today, scientists can work out what causes most diseases, but they cannot stop all dangerous diseases. People have to continue to find cures and adapt their lifestyles to fight the diseases that face them today.

AVIAN (BIRD) FLU

Avian flu exists worldwide and can infect other mammals as well as birds. Between 2003 and 2005, tens of millions of birds in Southeast Asia died from bird flu. Hundreds of millions more were killed to protect humans from infection. Yet over a hundred people in several countries caught bird flu. About half of them died.

TIMELINE

Early 1300s	Probable outbreak of the plague in inner Asia.
1330s	Rains, droughts, and earthquakes in China. The plague begins to spread.
1337	Hundred Years' War between England and France begins.
1346	The plague hits cities near the Caspian Sea.
1347	The plague attacks the Crimea, Greece, Sardinia, and Corsica.
Oct	The plague arrives in Messina, Sicily.
Nov	The plague hits Marseille, France.
1348	The plague reaches Spain and Austria. The Flagellant movement begins.
Jan	The plague reaches Genoa and Venice in Italy.
Mar	Florence is hit.
Jun	Plague in Paris. Plague arrives in England.
Aug	Plague attacks Rome.
Sep	Plague reaches London.
Nov	Pogroms against Jews begin in Germany.
1349	The plague hits Germany, Portugal, Norway, Sweden, Denmark, and the Netherlands. Pogroms against Jews in central Europe.

April	Black Death reaches Wales.
July	Black Death hits Ireland.
Oct	The pope excommunicates many of the Flagellants.
1350	Flagellant movement vanishes.
Spring	Plague reaches Scotland.
1351	Plague in Poland.
	The end of the Black Death in western Europe.
1352	Plague in Russia.
1361	The "children's plague" breaks out in Europe.
1381	Peasants' Revolt in England. There are also two more outbreaks of plague within this decade.
1400s	There were further outbreaks of plague in the first half of this century.
1453	The end of the Hundred Years' War.
1563	Queen Elizabeth I takes action during a plague outbreak that starts that year. She again takes action in a further outbreak in 1578.
1665	The last major plague outbreak in London.
1720s	The end of the plague in Europe.

GLOSSARY

abbot man in charge of a community of monks

antibiotics medicines that fight bacteria that can cause infections

ancestors all the past members of a family

archaeologist person who studies things left in the ground by people in the past

astrology study of stars and planets and how their movement may affect people's lives

bacillus type of bacteria, tiny living things that can cause disease

bloodletting cutting the skin to let blood flow out. This was used as a medical treatment.

bubo swollen lymph gland in the armpit or groin

bubonic type of plague spread through contact with rat fleas. It usually killed a person in less than a week.

chamber pot bowl-shaped container used like a toilet (potty)

chronicle written record of events in the order they happened

chronicler person who writes a chronicle

confess tell someone the bad things you have done so that you can be forgiven

dysentery bad infection in the stomach and intestines that causes diarrhoea and loss of blood

excommunicate banish someone from the Church. People feared that they then would not be allowed into heaven.

excrement solid waste that is passed out of a person's body

flagellant person who whips him or herself. Some eastern religions and certain Shia Muslim groups still practise flagellation.

fresco picture painted on a wall while the plaster is still wet

galley long, low ship often used for war and trading during the Middle Ages

Genoese people or ships whose home or home port is Genoa in Italy

host animal or plant that another animal or plant lives and feeds off

immune when a body is able to avoid getting an illness because it had the disease before and managed to get better

influenza like a very bad cold, flu causes fevers, pain, and weakness

lance to cut open an infected part of the body to let out the pus

latrine hole in the ground used as a toilet

lymph gland part of the body that helps fight infection and swells when it is doing so

mortality death

offal inside parts of an animal such as the intestine, liver, and heart

peasant farmer who works the land for a living

persecution treating people in a cruel way because of their religion, race, or beliefs

physician doctor

pneumonia illness that causes the lungs to become infected and inflamed (puffy and red), making it difficult to breathe

pneumonic type of plague that infects the lungs. People can spread the disease directly to each other through coughing.

pogrom organized killing of a group of people because of their race or religion

poll tax tax everyone has to pay. Each person has to pay the same amount.

septicaemic type of plague that attacks the bloodstream. There is bleeding into the skin and organs, causing black patches on the skin.

sewage pit deep hole that contains liquid and solid waste from humans

smallpox serious infectious disease that causes fever, marks on the skin, and death

tenant farmer farmer in medieval times who worked the land belonging to a landowner. He had to give a share of his produce to the landowner.

treatise long and serious piece of writing on a subject

typhus serious infectious disease that causes fever, headaches, purple marks on the body, and death

virus small, non-living thing that infects cells and can cause disease

woodcut print made from a pattern cut in a piece of wood

FINDING OUT MORE

BOOKS

A Painful History of Medicine Read titles such as *Scalpels, Stitches & Scars* and *Pox, Pus & Plague,* John Townsend (Raintree, 2006)

Art in History: Art of the Middle Ages, Jennifer Olmsted (Heinemann Library, 2006)

Body Talk: Defend Yourself, Steve Parker (Raintree, 2006)

Digging Deeper: Britain 1066–1500, Alan Brooks-Tyreman et al (Heinemann Library, 2006)

History of Britain: Medieval Britain, Brenda Williams (Heinemann Library, 2006)

Rat, Stephen Savage (Hodder Wayland, 2004)

The Black Death, Philip Ziegler (Sutton Publishing, 2003)
This is a good book for teachers.

Turning Points in History: Penicillin, Richard Tames (Heinemann Library, 2006)

PLACES TO VISIT

The Museum of London, London
www. museumoflondon.org.uk
Has galleries showing life in medieval London.

Weald and Downland Open Museum, Sussex
www.wealddown.co.uk
Historic buildings, some from the Middle Ages, show you what it was like to live in those times.

BLACK DEATH ONLINE

www.bbc.co.uk/history/society_culture/welfare/blacksocial_01.shtml
Find out about the plague in the UK on the BBC site.

www.themiddleages.net/life/blackdeath
Read about the Black Death as a news report.

en.wikipedia.org/wiki/Spanish_Flu
Learn about the outbreaks of Spanish Flu.

en.wikipedia.org/wiki/Great_Plague_of_London
Learn about the last major outbreak of plague in London.

www.historylearningsite.co.uk/plague_of_1665.htm
Read about the hardships of poor people in London at this time.

FURTHER RESEARCH

If you are interested in finding out more about the Black Death, try researching the following topics:

- how art from the Middle Ages teaches us about medieval life
- health and medicine in the Middle Ages
- the development of modern medicine
- how medicines, such as penicillin, fight disease
- modern diseases, such as AIDS, and how to prevent them.

INDEX

Titles in the *When Disaster Struck* series include:

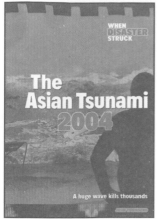

Hardback 1 406 20291 6

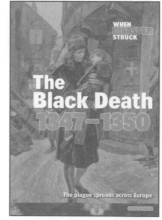

Hardback 1 406 20286 X

Hardback 1 406 20287 8

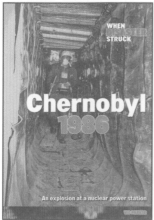

Hardback 1 406 20285 1

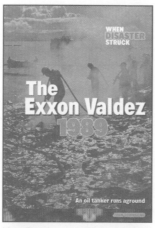

Hardback 1 406 20292 4

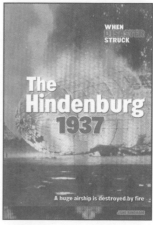

Hardback 1 406 20293 2

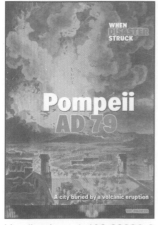

Hardback 1 406 20290 8

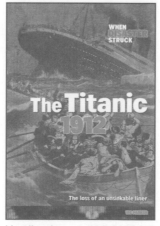

Hardback 1 406 20288 6

Find out about other titles from Raintree on our website www.raintreepublishers.co.uk